MEET
COOPER KUPP

KEITH ELLIOT GREENBERG

Lerner Publications ◆ Minneapolis

Free Database Trial: lernersports.com

Copyright © 2023 by Lerner Publishing Group, Inc.

All rights reserved. International copyright secured. No part of this book may be reproduced, stored in a retrieval system, or transmitted in any form or by any means—electronic, mechanical, photocopying, recording, or otherwise—without the prior written permission of Lerner Publishing Group, Inc., except for the inclusion of brief quotations in an acknowledged review.

Lerner Publications Company
An imprint of Lerner Publishing Group, Inc.
241 First Avenue North
Minneapolis, MN 55401 USA

For reading levels and more information, look up this title at www.lernerbooks.com.

Main body text set in Aptifer Slab LT Pro. Typeface provided by Linotype AG.

Editor: Matt Doeden

Library of Congress Cataloging-in-Publication Data

Names: Greenberg, Keith Elliot, 1959– author.
Title: Meet Cooper Kupp / Keith Elliot Greenberg.
Description: Minneapolis : Lerner Publications, 2023. | Series: Sports vips. Lerner sports | Includes bibliographical references and index. | Audience: Ages 7–11 | Audience: Grades 4–6 | Summary: "In 2021, Los Angeles Rams wide receiver Cooper Kupp led the NFL in catches and receiving yards. Then he led the Rams to victory in the Super Bowl. Learn about Kupp's life and athletic achievements"— Provided by publisher.
Identifiers: LCCN 2022020159 (print) | LCCN 2022020160 (ebook) | ISBN 9781728476025 (library binding) | ISBN 9781728478623 (paperback) | ISBN 9781728484983 (ebook)
Subjects: LCSH: Kupp, Cooper, 1993– | Football players—United States—Biography.
Classification: LCC GV939.K87 G74 2023 (print) | LCC GV939.K87 (ebook) | DDC 796.33092 [B]—dc23/eng/20220630

LC record available at https://lccn.loc.gov/2022020159
LC ebook record available at https://lccn.loc.gov/2022020160

Manufactured in the United States of America
1-52170-50632-8/4/2022

TABLE OF CONTENTS

SUPER BOWL MVP 4
FAST FACTS 5

CHAPTER 1
BORN FOR GREATNESS 8

CHAPTER 2
COLLEGE STAR 12

CHAPTER 3
WELCOME TO THE NFL 16

CHAPTER 4
A SENSE OF PURPOSE 22

COOPER KUPP CAREER STATS 28
GLOSSARY 29
SOURCE NOTES 30
LEARN MORE 31
INDEX 32

SUPER BOWL MVP

The Los Angeles Rams trailed the Cincinnati Bengals 20–16 in Super Bowl LVI. A little more than three minutes remained in the game. Rams quarterback Matthew Stafford took the ball. He knew what he had to do to turn the game around.

He needed to throw the ball to his star wide receiver, Cooper Kupp.

Because the Super Bowl was on the Rams' home field, the crowd was loudly cheering for the team. Most of them felt the same way as Stafford. They chanted the wide receiver's name.

FAST FACTS

DATE OF BIRTH: June 15, 1993
POSITION: wide receiver
LEAGUE: National Football League (NFL)

PROFESSIONAL HIGHLIGHTS: 2021 Offensive Player of the Year; 2021 winner of the Triple Crown; MVP of Super Bowl LVI

PERSONAL HIGHLIGHTS: was an honors student in high school; met his wife, Anna, while in high school; his father and grandfather both played in the NFL

Kupp prepares to catch a pass from Matthew Stafford during Super Bowl LVI.

Stafford seemed to be guided by the fans' voices. The next time the ball was in his hands, he looked away from his best pass catcher. But Kupp raced across the field and put himself in position. Then, while Stafford's eyes still appeared to be on something else, he fired the ball 22 yards right into Kupp's arms. The Rams were one yard away from winning the biggest game in football.

In the crowd, Kupp's parents and grandparents sat with his wife, Anna. Even his young children—three-year-old son, Cooper Jr., and one-year-old son, Cypress—seemed to be paying attention. They all wanted Kupp to get the ball and score.

Stafford took the snap. Cornerback Eli Apple was guarding Kupp. The receiver started up the field into the end zone. Apple followed. Then Kupp quickly changed directions, taking off toward the sideline. Stafford threw the ball. Kupp reached up and grabbed it at just the right time. Touchdown! The Rams took the lead and never looked back. The crowd roared.

In the game, Kupp caught eight passes for 92 yards and two touchdowns. His amazing performance earned him honors as the game's Most Valuable Player (MVP).

"He's been such a special player," said his coach, Sean McVay. "Love Cooper Kupp."

Kupp celebrates with his teammates after scoring the go-ahead touchdown in the fourth quarter of Super Bowl LVI.

CHAPTER 1

BORN FOR GREATNESS

Cooper Kupp was born on June 15, 1993, in Yakima, Washington. His parents almost named him Cody. But his father, Craig, changed his mind. He liked the name Cooper because he thought it would sound good over a loudspeaker. He expected his son to be a star.

Cooper grew up with his siblings, Ketner, Katrina, and Kobe. Sports were an important part of the family's life. Cooper's mother, Karin, had been a college soccer star. His dad had briefly played in the National Football League (NFL) as a quarterback. His grandfather Jake had also spent time in the NFL.

"We don't have many family gatherings where there isn't a football around somewhere," Kupp said.

Craig Kupp accepts the Jerry Rice Award for his son Cooper in 2013. The award goes to the most outstanding freshman in the Football Champion Subdivision (FCS).

Just as his father and grandfather had, Cooper also wanted to be a player in the NFL. To help achieve his dreams, he wrote down his goals for football and hung them up in his room.

When he started A.C. Davis High School, Cooper was small for his age. In a hard-hitting game like football, bigger, stronger players often have an advantage. Cooper secretly put on leg weights before the school's football coaches weighed him so they wouldn't know how small he was. As time went on, Kupp added muscle and size.

Kupp evades a tackle during a 2013 game between Eastern Washington University (EWU) and Montana.

Kupp also excelled in basketball. But football was what he loved the most. His speed and quickness made him difficult for defenders to catch. He was great at earning yards after catch (YAC). As a senior, he set a school record with 22 touchdowns.

Kupp said his biggest achievement that year was meeting Anna Croskey at a track meet. When he came home that day, he told his mother that he knew who he was going to marry.

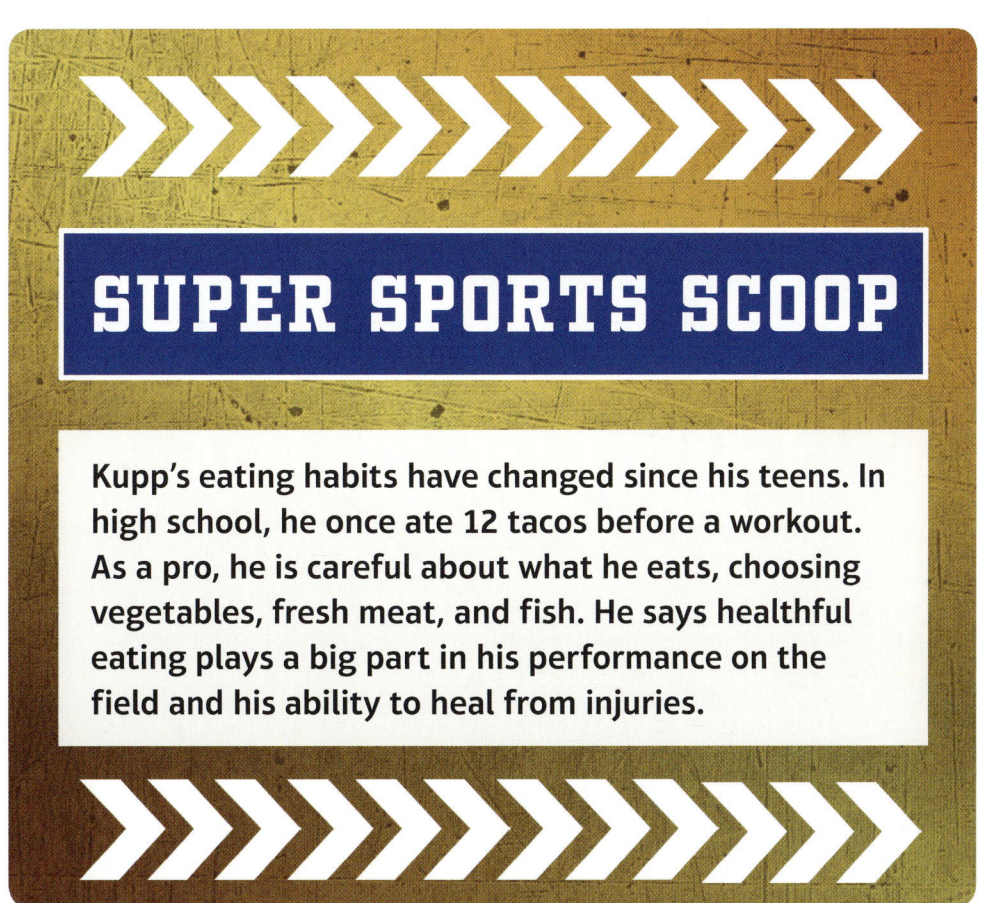

SUPER SPORTS SCOOP

Kupp's eating habits have changed since his teens. In high school, he once ate 12 tacos before a workout. As a pro, he is careful about what he eats, choosing vegetables, fresh meat, and fish. He says healthful eating plays a big part in his performance on the field and his ability to heal from injuries.

CHAPTER 2

COLLEGE STAR

Kupp played wide receiver and defensive back in high school. In 2011, his strong play earned him a scholarship offer from Eastern Washington University. EWU was part of the Football Championship Subdivision. It's the second-highest level of competition in college football

Kupp's play at EWU drew attention right away. In 2013, Kupp won the award for Best Freshman Player. In 2015, as a junior, he set the FCS record for catches, with 114. That season, he was honored with the Walter Payton Award, which goes to the best player in the FCS.

Kupp played so well that some people expected him to go the NFL instead of completing his senior year at EWU. He chose to finish college.

Kupp runs the ball for EWU in a 2014 game against the University of Washington.

Cooper and Anna Kupp married in 2015. They are shown here in 2020 at the Ninth Annual NFL Honors ceremony.

As he had promised, he married Anna while in college. She had been a track-and-field star at the University of Arizona. She transferred to EWU so she and Kupp could be together.

As an athlete, Anna played a big role in supporting Kupp's training. The two exercised together. They watched videos of opposing teams to help Kupp prepare for games. She helped Cooper concentrate on achieving his dream of playing in the NFL.

Their hard work paid off. Kupp was named All-American in each of his four college seasons and piled up records along the way. His 428 receptions and 6,464 yards were the most in FCS history.

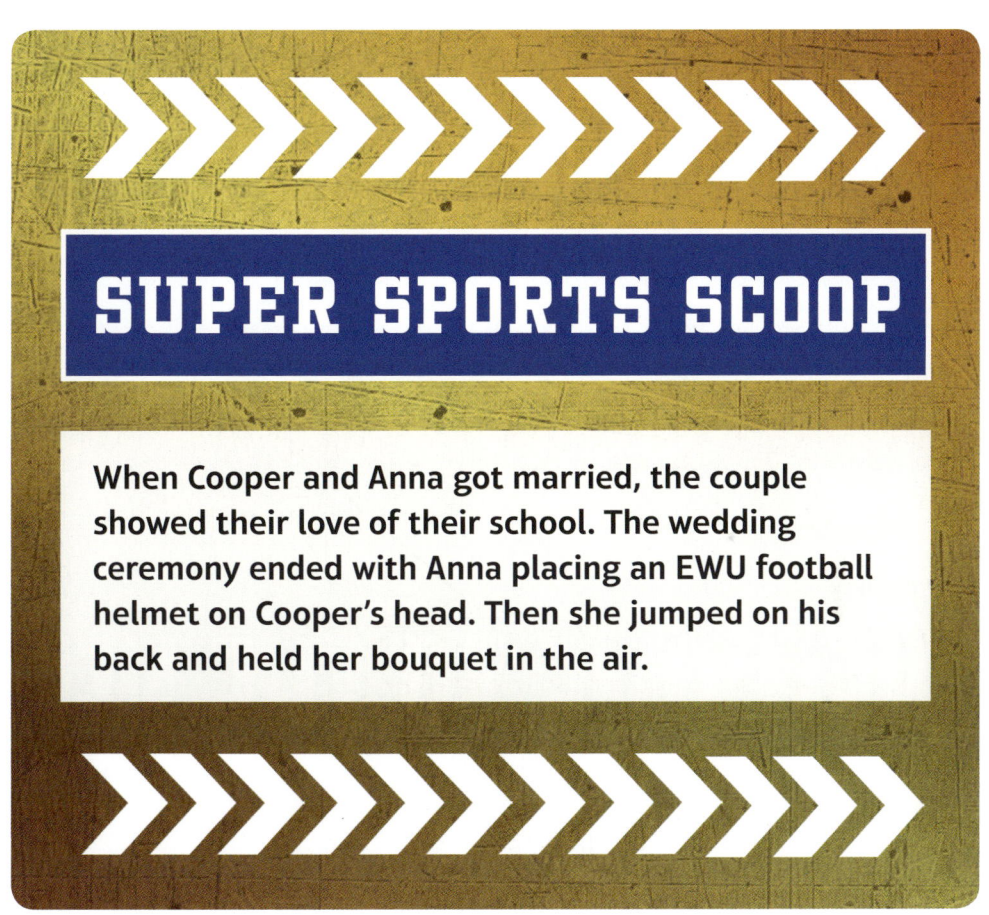

SUPER SPORTS SCOOP

When Cooper and Anna got married, the couple showed their love of their school. The wedding ceremony ended with Anna placing an EWU football helmet on Cooper's head. Then she jumped on his back and held her bouquet in the air.

CHAPTER 3

WELCOME TO THE NFL

Often, FCS players are overlooked by pro scouts. The scouts tend to focus most of their attention on the top level of college competition. But Kupp's achievements left no doubt that he was bound for the NFL. One draft expert called him "as natural a pass catcher as you will find."

As teams gathered for the 2017 NFL Draft, Kupp watched eagerly. The first two rounds came and went. Finally, in the third round, the Los Angeles Rams called his name. Kupp was thrilled. His dream was coming true!

As a rookie, Kupp became close friends with Rams quarterback Jared Goff. The two watched films of other teams to better understand their opponents. They also went over the best plays to use in different situations.

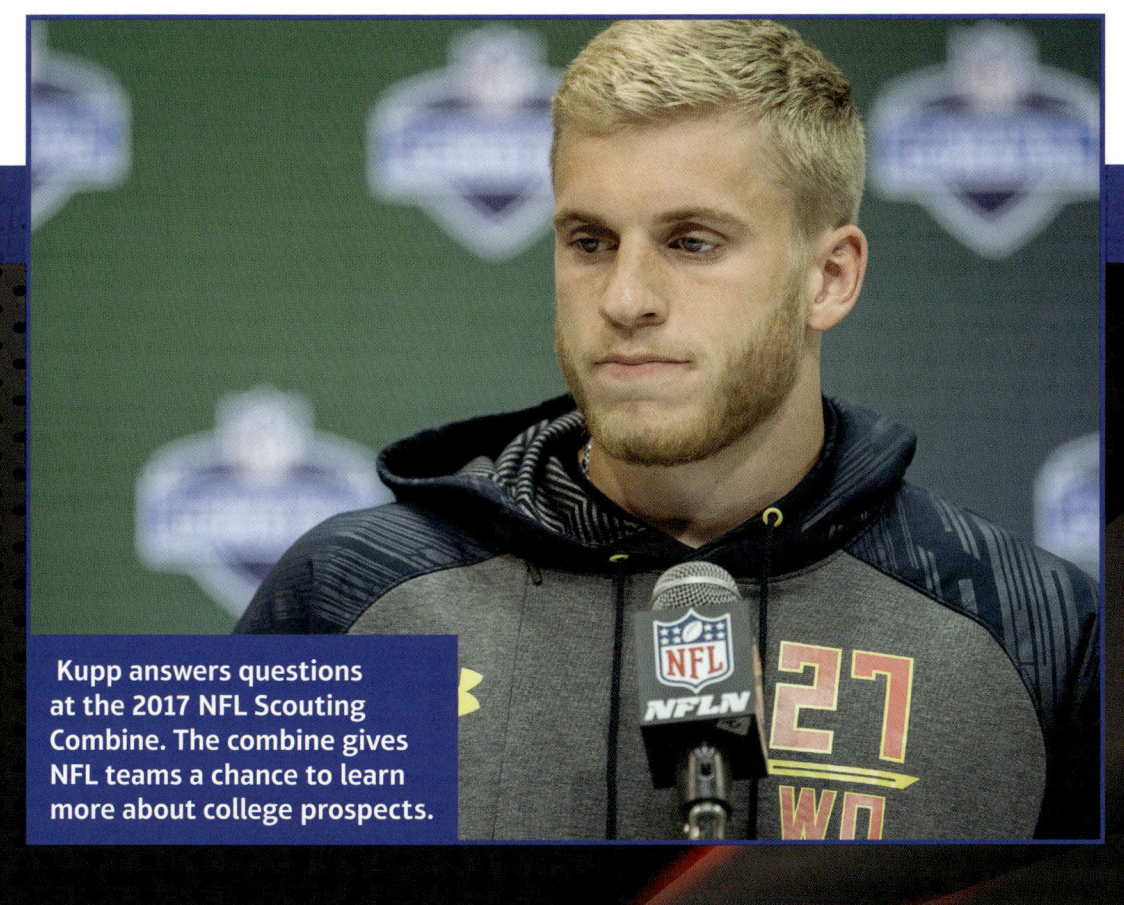

Kupp answers questions at the 2017 NFL Scouting Combine. The combine gives NFL teams a chance to learn more about college prospects.

In his first game as an NFL player, Kupp caught four passes and scored a touchdown. The Rams beat the Indianapolis Colts 46–9.

With each game, Kupp learned and improved. At the end of the season, the Rams had a record of 11–5 and went to the playoffs. Kupp caught eight passes and ran for 69 yards in his playoff debut. But the Rams lost to the Atlanta Falcons.

Kupp runs with the ball in a game against the Jacksonville Jaguars in 2017.

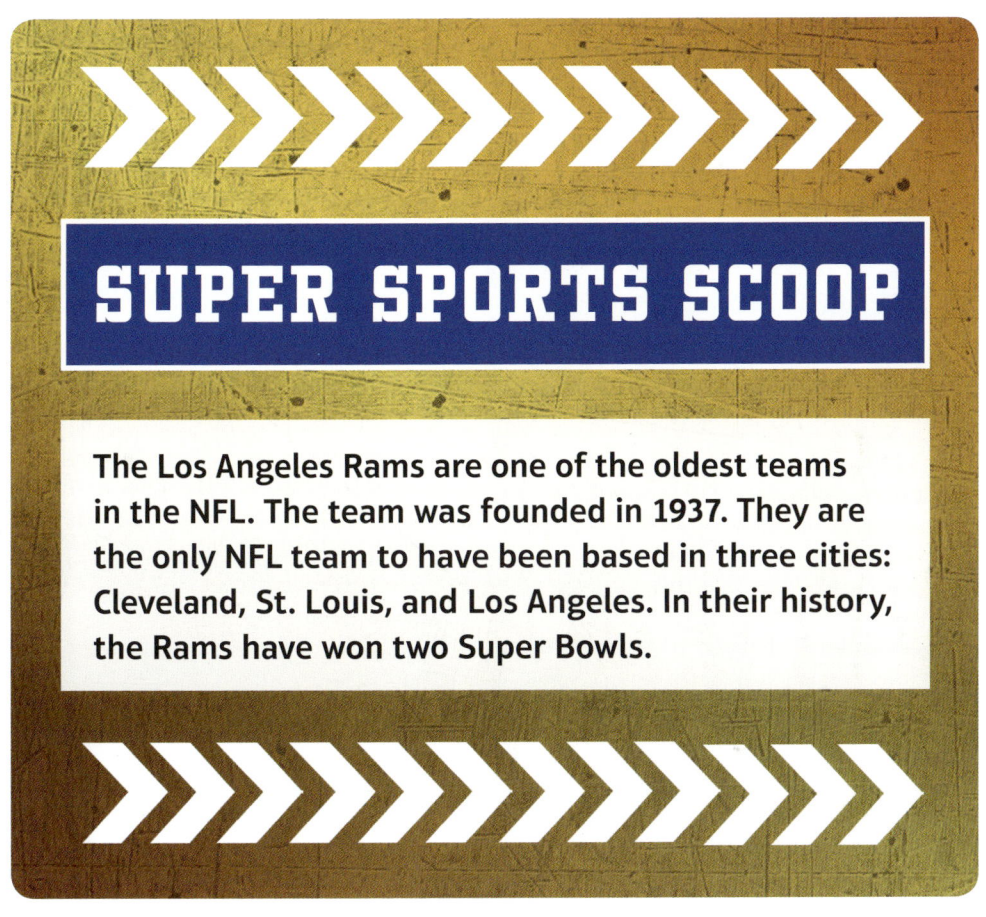

SUPER SPORTS SCOOP

The Los Angeles Rams are one of the oldest teams in the NFL. The team was founded in 1937. They are the only NFL team to have been based in three cities: Cleveland, St. Louis, and Los Angeles. In their history, the Rams have won two Super Bowls.

Kupp's 2018 season ended early. In a game against the Seattle Seahawks, he was running across the field when he went down, holding his left knee. It was bad news. Kupp had torn a ligament. The serious injury required surgery and a recovery time of six to nine months.

All Kupp wanted to do was play football. But first, he had to learn how to run again. He worked with specialists and watched films of himself in slow motion, studying every stride. His hard work was worth the effort. The knee healed, and Kupp was even faster than before.

Kupp is off to the races after catching a pass in his NFL debut in 2017.

Kupp returned to action in 2019. Here, he hauls in a pass against the Baltimore Ravens.

When the 2019 season began, Kupp scored a touchdown in each of the Rams' first four games. He finished the year as the team's leader in receptions, receiving yards, and receiving touchdowns.

Kupp was on his way to becoming a superstar. But even bigger things were ahead.

CHAPTER 4

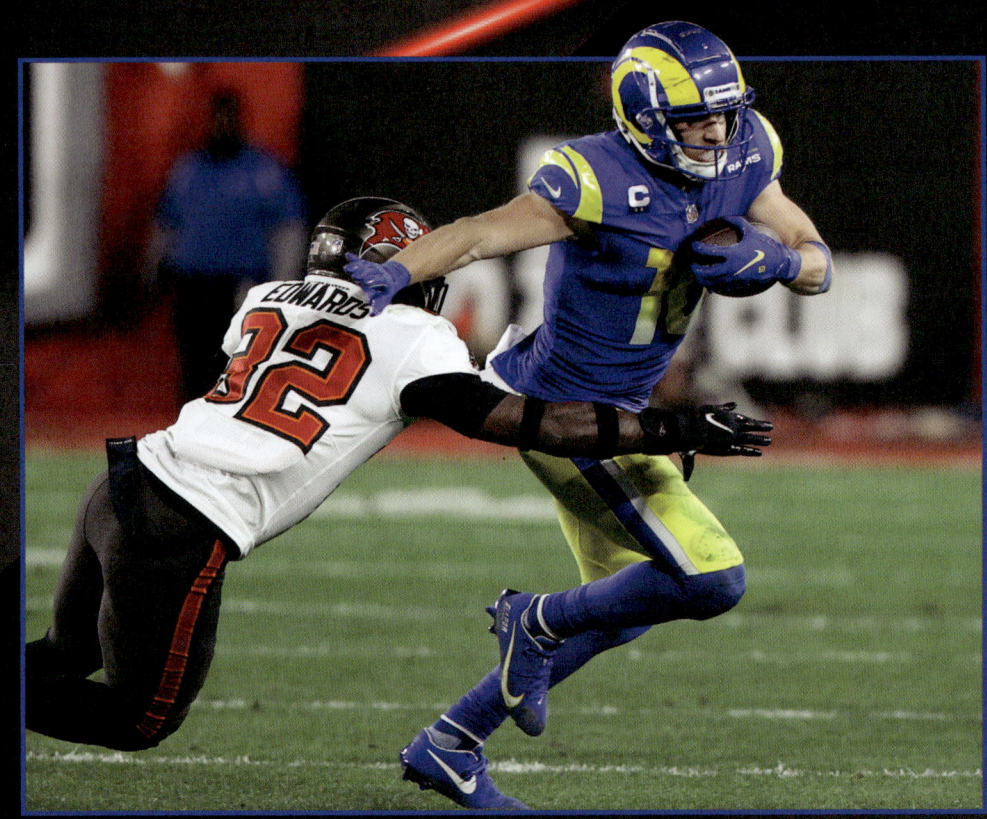

A SENSE OF PURPOSE

The year Kupp was injured, the Rams were in the Super Bowl. Kupp was unable to play in the game, and his team lost to the New England Patriots. At a press conference after the game, Kupp said he had a vision that one day in the future, he "was going to walk off the Super Bowl field as the MVP."

After the 2020 season, the Rams traded Goff and some draft choices to the Detroit Lions for quarterback Matthew Stafford. Kupp quickly befriended his new teammate. Throughout the season, they met for breakfast to talk about game strategies. Because of their close connection, they went into each game with a deep understanding of how to work together.

Kupp celebrates a touchdown with Jared Goff in 2020. Goff was traded to Detroit after the season.

Kupp blows past the Tampa Bay defense during a 2022 playoff game. The Rams won the game, 30–27.

The Rams finished the season with a record of 12–5. Kupp broke a team record with 145 receptions for 1,947 yards. With his playoff totals added, Kupp became the first wide receiver in history to total more than 2,000 receiving yards.

In the playoffs, the Rams beat the Arizona Cardinals, Tampa Bay Buccaneers, and San Francisco 49ers to earn their spot in the 2021 Super Bowl.

In the biggest game of the year, Stafford and Kupp were unstoppable against a tough Cincinnati Bengals defense. In the second quarter, Kupp got away from his defender and grabbed a touchdown in the right corner of the end zone. In total, he caught eight passes for 92 yards, including the game-winning touchdown.

SUPER SPORTS SCOOP

Kupp believes in using his fame to help other people. His favorite charities include organizations that provide food for people in need. He also helps fund scholarships for students.

Kupp streaks across the middle of the field after catching a pass in Super Bowl LVI.

For the first time since 2000, the Rams were champions. At the end of the game, the Kupp and Stafford families rushed toward each other. "There was a lot of high-fives," said Craig Kupp, "a lot of hugs, a lot of tears."

As Cooper had predicted, he was the Super Bowl MVP. His vision of winning it all had come true.

At the press conference after the game, Kupp said that his family's support had been very important. He also spoke about the respect he had for his teammates. "It's just been the perfect team, the perfect setup," he said. "And I'm so thankful for everyone that's been around me. It still really hasn't hit me."

Kupp was grateful for the chance to be a Super Bowl hero. His fans hope to see him back in the big game many times in the years to come.

Kupp celebrates with his wife, Anna, and their kids after beating the Bengals in Super Bowl LVI.

COOPER KUPP CAREER STATS

CAREER COLLEGE RECEPTIONS:
428

NFL RECEPTIONS:
433

CAREER COLLEGE RECEIVING YARDS:
6,464

NFL TOUCHDOWNS:
40

CAREER COLLEGE TOUCHDOWNS:
73

NFL POSTSEASON TOUCHDOWNS:
7

Stats are accurate through the 2021 NFL season.

GLOSSARY

All-American: an honor given to the top athletes at their position each college season

draft: the system by which NFL teams select new, incoming college players

ligament: a band of tough, flexible tissue that connects two bones

rookie: a first-year player

scholarship: money given to a student to help pay for their education

scout: someone who evaluates prospects to determine how successful they might be at the next level

yards after catch: a stat that measures how far a receiver runs after catching the ball

SOURCE NOTES

7   Lindsey Thiry, "The Making of Cooper Kupp: Los Angeles Rams Receiver Credits Wife's Inspiration for Superstar Turn," *ESPN*, February 12, 2022, https://www.espn.com/nfl/story/_/id/33109684/the-making-cooper-kupp-los-angeles-rams-receiver-credits-wife-inspiration-superstar-turn.

9   Roger Underwood, "Yakima Valley's First Family of Football: Cooper Kupp Likely to Be Third Generation NFL Player," *Yakima (WA) Herald-Republic*, October 22, 2016, https://www.yakimaherald.com/sports/college_sports/yakima-valleys-first-family-of-football|-cooper-kupp-likely-to-be-third-generation-nfl-player/article_df1ef380-98a8-11e6-81c3-67f4724d8327.html.

16   "Cooper Kupp," NFL.com, accessed August 3, 2022, https://www.nfl.com/prospects/cooper-kupp/32004b55-5053-4597-b958-87408c31956f.

22   Frank Schwab, "Cooper Kupp Had a Vision 3 Years Ago: Rams Winning the Super Bowl, with Him as SB MVP," Yahoo Sports, February 14, 2022, https://sports.yahoo.com/cooper-kupp-had-a-vision-3-years-ago-rams-winning-the-super-bowl-with-him-as-sb-mvp-062554141.html.

26   Steve Serby, "Inside Cooper Kupp's Unreal Super Bowl 2022 through His Parents' Eyes: 'Bedlam,'" *New York Post*, February 14, 2022, https://nypost.com/2022/02/14/inside-cooper-kupps-super-bowl-2022-through-his-parents-eyes/.

27   Stephen Holder, "How the Rams' Cooper Kupp's Quiet Vision Became Reality in Front of the Whole World," Athletic, February 14, 2022, https://theathletic.com/3128598/2022/02/14/how-the-rams-cooper-kupps-quiet-vision-became-reality-in-front-of-the-whole-world/.

LEARN MORE

Bankston, John. *Jared Goff*. Hallandale, FL: Mitchell Lane, 2018.

Cooper Kupp
https://cooperkupp.com

Morey, Allan. *The Los Angeles Rams Story*. Minneapolis: Bellwether Media, 2017.

NFL Players: Cooper Kupp
https://www.nfl.com/players/cooper-kupp/

Scheff, Matt. *Matthew Stafford*. Lake Elmo, MN: Focus Readers, 2023.

Sports Illustrated Kids: NFL Zone
https://www.sikids.com/nfl-zone

INDEX

A.C. Davis High School, 10–11

All-American, 15

Eastern Washington University (EWU), 12–15

Goff, Jared, 17, 23

injury, 11, 19, 22

Kupp, Anna, 5–6, 11, 14–15

Kupp, Craig, 5, 8–10

McVay, Sean, 7

NFL Draft, 17

rookie, 17

Stafford, Matthew, 4–7, 23, 25–26

Super Bowl, 4–7, 19, 22, 24–27

Walter Payton Award, 13

PHOTO ACKNOWLEDGMENTS

Image credits: AP Photo/Marcio Jose Sanchez, p. 4; Andy Lyons/Getty Images, pp. 6, 8, 26; Ronald Martinez/Getty Images, p. 7; Mitchell Leff/Getty Images, p. 9; AP Photo/Michael Albans, p. 10; AP Photo/Laura Dickinson, p. 12; AP Photo/Icon Sportsire/Joshua Weisberg, p. 13; AP Photo/Todd Rosenberg, p. 14; Meg Oliphant/Getty Images, p. 16; Zach Bolinger/Icon Sportswire/Getty Images, p. 17; Don Juan Moore/Getty Images, p. 18; Jeff Gross/Getty Images, p. 20; AP Photo/Jose Sanchez, p. 21; AP Photo/Mark LoMoglio, p. 22; Timothy T Ludwig/Getty Images, p. 23; AP Photo/Jason Behnken, p. 24; AP Photo/Ryan King, p. 27.

Design elements: The Hornbills Studio/Shutterstock; Tamjaii9/Shutterstock.

Cover: AP Photo/Nick Wass.